Calling
All
Canines...
And Their Owners

Calling All Canines...
And Their Owners

SHERI VENZA

Dog Trainer/Behaviorist

CALLING ALL CANINES

DOG TRAINING

www.CallingAllCanines.com

CALLING ALL CANINES

DOG TRAINING

Published by
Calling All Canines
Robbinsville, NJ 08691 USA
www.CallingAllCanines.com

Published 2012

ISBN 978-0-9850023-0-5

Library of Congress Control Number: 2012900169

Editor: Jean B. Taber
Cover design: Lara Jean Taber
Illustrations: Mary Vaughan
Book layout: Pat Gaudette

Printed in the United States of America

*A special 'thank you' to Lara Taber
without whom this book would not exist.*

Contents

INTRODUCTION

Hello and welcome to *Calling All Canines... and Their Owners!* I'd like to introduce you to my method of dog training – training the way Mother Nature intended it – without the use of food motivation, toys, or other unnecessary gadgets.

This book is the result of more than 20 years of experience with dog behaviorism and training in homes, and with what people seemed to need the most.

It's an easy-to-read quick reference book that addresses common behaviors that dogs exhibit and what to do about them.

As a behaviorist, I want to emphasize that dogs do *everything* for a reason – or a combination of reasons. This belief is the foundation upon which formal training is then built.

A dog needs to see his owner as the "alpha" in its home territory. If not, he will be unable to do so in a more distracting outside atmosphere.

Training starts from the moment you bring your pet into your home.

When you understand *why* your dog thinks the way he does, training should and can be fun for you and the entire family as well as for your pet.

All dogs are pack animals. Big or small, they are wired like their cousin, the wolf. By nature, they exist and live according to the structure of the wolf pack.

Although they are all unique with their own individual personalities, some dogs are more dominate ,and some are more submissive. However, they are all fundamentally the same and need to be taught what you want and expect from them, in a manner they can instinctively understand.

You would never see the leader of a pack of dogs or wolves hand out "treats" to have the pack follow him!

When you use external stimuli for acquiring a response from a dog, you are teaching him to respond for a food reward and not out of an instinctive need to please the alpha dog.

Also, using food rewards is unhealthy for your dog, contributing to obesity and inhibiting the housebreaking training process.

Cause and effect – your pet does this, and that happens. Your dog gets positive reinforcement of the appropriate behavior so he is able to learn what behaviors you want and expect from him.

Your puppy or older dog has an instinctive need to please you, looking to you as the leader of the pack.

Dogs are very smart but also very simple – either he is the boss or you are. Once your pet respects you, he respects everything associated with you – your home, your children, and so on.

My methods are structured according to how a dog thinks instinctively and coincide with real life situations: people with jobs, kids, visitors, different schedules, etc.

This is reality training and requires consistency, repetition and commitment. The more consistent an owner is, the sooner the dog learns what is expected. It takes time, but time that pays off for the rest of the dog's life with you.

Believe it or not, people treat dogs like people, and dogs treat people like dogs! This book will help you bridge that communication gap between human and pack animal by giving you the tools to understand your dog.

Fun, fair but firm, structured interaction with your dog, and the means to promote the wanted behaviors are the goals of this book.

Congratulations on your pet choice, and happy reading!

BRINGING YOUR PUPPY HOME

Be prepared. Know what to do, why to do it, and, most importantly, *how* to do it before you bring your dog home.

Puppies and dogs do not come pre-programmed knowing what to do in OUR world. They are animals that like to pee on the floor and outside because they are wired like the wolf and follow their instincts.

Even though we have domesticated them, a dog is a dog is a dog. Dogs see life only from a pack perspective, not from the human, or people, perspective. They need to be treated like the dogs they are, but they are capable of being taught what is expected in the world of people.

Dogs are smart and the rules of the pack are simple.

As early as four-five weeks of age, in a litter of puppies, a hierarchy is established from alpha to beta and down the ladder to omega, with every dog having his spot on that ladder.

According to the dog's position on the ladder, there is a very clear understanding of what is or is not allowed.

The alpha, or top dog, is the leader of the pack. The alpha dog makes all the decisions for the rest of the litter.

When we touch a dog, even if we are correcting him, we are inadvertently praising him.

Touch is praise, pure and simple. He is confused because he sees your body language and hears your tone, yet he thinks he is being praised.

The dog becomes stressed, exhibiting what we consider "bad" behavior. The cycle becomes more and more frustrating for both the owner and the pet.

I can't tell you how many times I have heard a person say, "The dog knows he did something wrong."

No, the dog is usually responding to body language and tone and showing submissive body language. He does not know why his owner is mad and certainly does not understand what the behavior was that made his owner angry.

Puppies and dogs need to be taught what is expected of them according to their world and understanding. They are incapable of thinking like us; we have to think like them.

There are no hidden trainer secrets. It is simply a question of having the correct knowledge and knowing how to apply it successfully.

Dog training should be fun for owner and dog alike, a pleasant, happy experience for everyone including the pet.

Just remember, you have to think like a dog and treat him in a manner he understands so he will learn how to fit into your home, life, and schedule.

The most important point is for your dog to know who is in command or who is the "alpha." It does not matter to him if it is you or he, but he needs to know who is in charge.

Once you have implemented and reinforced your dominance, you will have a stress-free, calm, happy addition to your family.

The benefit for you is a well-trained, well-mannered, well-behaved dog, and for the dog it provides a stress-free, happy, calm, and secure environment.

At eight weeks of age, the day you bring your puppy into the house he is *waiting* to be shown where he belongs in his new "pack" – your family.

The first mistake people make when they bring their puppy home is to lavish love on their cute new fluff ball.

Let's face it, who doesn't melt at the sight of a puppy?

The translation from the puppy's perspective: "OK, all the subordinates are lavishing attention on me, so I must be the alpha because the rest of the pack only submits to the alpha."

Instead, you should roll the puppy gently on his back and place your hand gently around his neck until he stops resisting and moving. Immediately release your hand from your puppy's neck as you praise him.

Do not use high-pitched baby talk as this mimics another puppy or litter-mate to your dog. Be firm but happy.

For your dog this is like a "dominant down," which is how a dominant member of the pack reinforces his or her position as the alpha over the new member of the pack.

Your puppy will instinctively understand as this is how one dog corrects or dominates another.

If you have an older, stronger dog and it could be a struggle, *do not attempt this method*. It will only reinforce what your dog sees as a struggle within the hierarchy for position in the pack.

This "dominant down" is only for young, easily manageable puppies.

You should place a soft nylon collar with a belt – not a snap – closure on your puppy so that you can fit two fingers flat between the neck and the collar.

Some toy and long-necked dogs such as the whippet and the greyhound need to have a martingale or harness due to the fragility of their trachea. Check with your vet first.

Attach a leash and let your puppy drag it around in the house, so you are never without a way to correct or control him in a way he understands.

Remember, *touch is praise*! You never see a dog pick up a paw or rolled up newspaper and whack or smack another dog. When you do this it only creates mistrust of you, and can prompt a pain or defensive reaction from your dog.

A firm, gentle pull on the leash as you firmly say "no" will let your puppy instinctively know you are correcting him.

Never use your dog's name when you are correcting him as the dog then gets a negative association with his name.

Only use your dog's name when you are praising him so he will like his name and will want to respond to it.

After a correction, always praise the puppy for the correct behavior so he learns what you want from him.

For example, if your puppy nips, that is not tolerable behavior. Even though he is teething, that is not why he is using you as a chew toy.

A firm "no" and a gentle pull on the leash lets you accomplish what you need to do. Then give the puppy one of his bones and tell him he's a good boy.

You have about 10 seconds before your puppy forgets, so consistency, repetition and commitment are key.

MATURING

It is a total fallacy that one year of a dog's life is equal to seven human years. Your eight-week-old dog is *not* the dog you will have at six months.

All dogs between the ages of six to nine months enter their adolescent years. Just like human teenagers, they will test the boundaries and structure put in place to see what they can get away with.

Your dog looks to you to exhibit alpha leadership qualities in order to ensure the entire "pack's" survival. In this way all breeds, from toy poodle to Rottweiler, are fundamentally the same.

Just as the human child must first crawl, then walk, and then run, so too all dogs must develop the way Mother Nature intended.

A female dog, regardless of breed, is in its adolescent stage from six to nine months through 18 months.

A male dog is an adolescent for a minimum of two years, and sometimes longer, depending on the breed and size.

As long as you reprimand your dog in a consistent manner when he "tests" you throughout adolescence, you will have set the foundation for the next 10+ years of his life.

A dog does not outgrow puppy behaviors. Bad puppy behaviors turn into bad adult dog behaviors.

If you allow this to happen, you will have to re-train and re-condition him. It can be done, but it will take extra time and effort.

BASIC HOME
INFORMATION

Dogs do *everything* for a reason. Jumping, nipping (teething, as some of my clients like to explain), are all inappropriate behaviors by a subordinate pack member toward a dominant pack member.

Dogs don't see life as sometimes you are the boss and other times you are a playmate. They are very black and white about it – either you are the boss or you're not.

You *never* see the alpha dog playing with other subordinate members of the pack.

You should never roughhouse or have a tug-of-war with a dog.

Even though you are playing, there are other behavioral issues going on. Your dog thinks, if it is okay to play and bite *your* hands, then it is okay to do it to all people.

"Playing" with a dog, such as tug-of-war, is seen as a dominance challenge by the dog. Even if he never wins, this can promote unwanted challenging behavior as well as potential aggression.

When a dog sees you as the leader of the pack, he believes that what is his is yours. There is no challenge, *ever*.

By promoting challenge, you are promoting a struggle for leadership within your "pack."

Either a dog may or may not do something; there is no gray area. Tug-of-war is always a struggle for leadership; it teaches your dog to challenge you.

Not everyone likes dogs and some people are even afraid of them.

If a person pulls his arm or hand back when the dog is "playing," you can be sued for having a "bad" dog that you created.

You inadvertently taught your dog to interact that way with other people by playing roughly with him.

When a dog jumps, people think he is excited and can't help himself. Yes, the dog *is* excited but he is also stressed. Here's why: within five seconds of a dog meeting a person (whom he thinks of as another dog) he must immediately determine who is "alpha" over whom.

The dog jumps, the person pets the dog (remember, touch is praise) and the dog thinks he is being praised for dominating.

Even if the dog is pushed away, he is still being touched and therefore still thinks he is being praised for being the one in charge.

Your dog should always have a leash and collar attached to him so you are never without a way to correct or control him.

When you grab the leash while his paws are off the floor and firmly tug it down as you say "no," he will instinctively understand this is the correction you mean it to be.

If you do not have a leash on your dog and grab the collar you are touching your dog's neck and therefore praising him.

When entering or leaving your home with your dog, he should always be on a leash held behind you. This way you are ALWAYS entering and exiting in front of him so he does not get the message that he is in charge of you.

The "alpha" dog is the ONLY dog that leads the pack.

JUMPING

When company comes to the door or a stranger approaches you and your dog, you should *not* let the person immediately touch your dog.

Let's go over the door issue first.

To properly teach your dog that you are in charge of who can or can't come into your territory, you must take the dog with you when someone comes to the door.

Before you open the door, step on your dog's leash. If he jumps, the leash will correct him since your dog is

causing his own discomfort and has no option but to remain calm and settle down.

Then you open the door and ask your guests to ignore your dog until he is calm.

Company coming and going in the dog's territory is every dog's nightmare. He is unable to sit or listen to your command until you have taught him you are in charge. When your dog has calmed down, he has absorbed the fact that someone is in his home.

You can now remove your foot from the leash. He is learning that he is the cause of his own distress and will learn to settle down as a result.

If your dog tries to jump on your guest, you must gently tug the leash when his paws leave the ground – but not before – and firmly say "no" at the same time. As soon as his paws hit the ground, you praise him.

In this way, your dog directly associates the correction with his behavior and not with your company. He has absorbed the fact that this person is in your home by the time you remove your foot from the leash.

Dogs are very literal, so you have to be precise – simple, but clear. This sets the foundation for a "sit/stay" at the door by first conditioning the dog that you are in charge at the door.

When you are out walking your dog, the same holds true. Dogs are instinctively leery of strangers.

Bending over the top of a dog, looking him directly in the eye, or reaching over the dog's head are all dominant actions, according to the dog's view of the world. To him, it is very stressful and threatening.

When your dog is calm he feels secure. Socialization for a dog means seeing other dogs, people, children, and cars, but always under your supervision and your control.

A dog does not know a bad stranger from a good stranger. It is imperative that your dog be responsible *to* you but not *for* you, especially with guard dogs and protective breeds.

The dog's instinct to protect you and your family is the same one that can get you in a world of trouble.

When a person approaches you and your dog, put your foot on the leash and explain that your dog is in training and you'd prefer he not be touched.

By putting your foot on the leash you have full immediate control and your dog understands that the situation is not threatening.

If you were with any small child and a stranger approached you and asked to hug your child, what would your first response be?

Why do people expect their dogs to be friendly to everyone? That is not how animals – and yes, especially dogs – are wired. They are instinctively leery of strangers, so they do what any pack alpha dog would do: they take on the role of boss.

Your dog must understand that he does not have the right to greet everyone he meets. You want him to be under your control and to remain calm in a "stay" position.

The same is true regarding meeting other dogs. Not all dogs are friendly. Two of the same gender who are both dominant will get into a dominance altercation. Within five seconds, one dog must submit to the other. If this does not occur, they will get into a tiff until one submits to the other.

Even if dogs know or grow up with each other, when they hit adolescence their instincts start to develop and mature. A six to nine month-old dog is comparable to having a teenager on your hands.

Throughout adolescence any dog, from a teacup Yorkie to a Great Dane, will test his boundaries and your leadership.

I have clients who are upset because they feed and love their dog, but then the dog nips them, jumps on them, or ignores them. The reason for this? Your dog needs a leader in order to feel secure; that is how you show love to your dog.

It is nothing personal. A dog's love and loyalty are unconditional and will not change. He would prefer not to have the burden of leadership, but if he sees what he perceives to be weaknesses, his instinct is to take charge.

So let's re-cap:

Even though we have domesticated them, dogs are instinctively wired like the wolf. They see life from the pack perspective.

Your dominance and leadership must be established not only for their sense of security and well being, but also so you will have a well-mannered, well-behaved dog that is a pleasure for you, your family, and other people to be around.

Not all people like dogs and some people are afraid of them.

Your family represents your dog's new pack. He needs to be taught immediately where he fits in.

He needs the consistency, repetition, mental stimulation, and yes, *fun*, of training.

Your dog is smart; he needs a job.

Socialization, training, walking, mental and physical exercise should all be done at once.

Frequent, short spurts are the best kind of training. And training must be done inside your home as well as outside.

If you do not work your dog indoors, you will only have a well-trained outside dog.

Tying your dog to a chain outdoors will ensure a future aggressive and unsocialized animal.

If you do not let bad behaviors or habits develop, you never have to fix them.

If you have provided a firm foundation from puppyhood through adolescence, your dog knows only the correct behavior and you get to enjoy your dog for the rest of his life with you.

In brief:

- Attach a leash to the dog prior to company arriving. Grabbing him by the collar still touches the dog, and touch is praise that reinforces bad behavior.

- Put your foot on the leash, up to the collar on the outside of the foot, prior to opening the door. This effortlessly and clearly implements immediate control since the dog is causing the tension and he has no option but to settle down.

- Do not let people approach or touch your dog until he has calmed down and you have removed your foot from the leash.

- Keep a leash loose, just enough slack to be able to immediately control and correct your dog at the time that behavior needs correcting.

- Correct at the time of the behavior not in anticipation of it.

- Say "no" and correct at the same time without the use of the dog's name.

- As soon as his paws are on the ground, praise him so he learns what you want and expect.

- **Do not allow your dog to jump sometimes but then correct him at other times.** Either the dog may or may not jump. Either a dog may or may not do something. Do not stress your dog by allowing this kind of confusion.

TOYS

Having the correct equipment and knowledge before you bring your dog home is half the work.

Dogs cannot tell the difference between your furniture, rugs and clothing, and their rope toys and stuffed animals.

Your children's stuffed animals look and feel the same to the puppy as its own stuffed animals.

Your dog needs hard, durable and *safe* dog toys to chew on, to offer him relief while teething as well as to prevent him from chewing up your house.

Giving him fabric-related, stuffy, fleecy, or wooly items conditions and trains your dog to chew up your household furnishings.

And there's also the safety issue. Puppies, like babies, will put everything in their mouths. They'll immediately chew on anything that looks interesting: wires, rocks, and plastic bottles that might contain ammonia, bleach, and other harmful cleansers and poisons kept in those containers.

To your dog, a plastic bottle with coins in it is the same thing as a container of harmful cleansers and poisons.

You are teaching your dog those items are okay when you give him a

plastic bottle as a toy; he simply cannot tell the difference.

Also dogs, like babies and toddlers, need constant supervision. A dog will become destructive because of boredom, stress, or frustration.

Remember, when your dog is never allowed to develop bad habits and behaviors, you never have to fix them.

If you teach your dog from Day One what he may and may not do, he won't know anything else.

Kong is one company whose *rubber* toys I recommend. Instead of filling them with soft fillers, I recommend hard kibbles of food or hard dog biscuits. This way there is no residual forming bacteria.

Ask your vet to recommend hard and durable dog toys that don't resemble anything in your home and are safe for your dog.

I encourage a toy rotation to keep your dog always stimulated.

Make three bags labeled 1, 2 and 3, with five toys per bag. On Day One the dog gets Bag One, Bag Two on Day Two, and Bag Three on Day Three. By the time you are on Day Four, your dog is back to Day One toys.

If he has all the toys all the time, he will get bored. A toy rotation makes your toys and money last longer, and every day will be like your dog's birthday!

In brief:

- Have three bags labeled 1, 2 and 3, with five toys per bag, to be rotated daily. Bag One on Day One, and so on. By Day Four back to Bag One; there will always be new toys to play with.

- I recommend Kong toys. Toys should not resemble anything in your home, nothing stuffy, fleecy, fabric-related, or old shoes. These types of toys teach your dog to chew items you don't want chewed and are hazardous to him.

IN THE HOUSE

Your dog should have **zero** unsupervised freedom until he learns what he may and may not have in your house.

A leash attached to your dog – yes, dragging around inside your house with you – is imperative in teaching your dog what he may and may not do and have.

When he goes for that wire, you grab the leash and gently but firmly tug on it as you say "no." Then hand him one of his toys and praise him. You have a ten-second window before your dog forgets; so again, you need that consistency.

Everything is by association with a dog. You want to establish the connection between "no" and discomfort in a manner he will understand.

He does not associate being smacked or hit with your hand or a rolled up newspaper with behavior correction. It only creates mistrust between you and your dog. He may even react in pain.

Remember that when we touch a dog, we are inadvertently praising him. He gets confused when you physically touch him for a correction.

A firm but gentle tug on the leash and a firm "no," without using your dog's name, teaches your dog in a manner he instinctively understands.

Only use your dog's name for praise and in happy, joyful tones. If you yell, he actually perceives you as a dog out of control!

Your dog wants to please you, so keep it simple. Correction followed by praise will reinforce the appropriate behavior you want your dog to learn.

Your puppy should not be "elevated in pack status" by being allowed on the furniture or the bed! This sends him the wrong message, that he is equal to you if he is sharing your space.

You may get down on the floor to his level to cuddle him, but it is confusing and stressful for him to think he has been raised up to your level.

Putting your dog on your furniture or bed can also contribute to potential future issues with anyone else sitting or sleeping in what he considers to be *his* space.

Your dog should always remain in a subordinate position and should, therefore, remain on the floor at all times. Buy him his own dog bed; there are many good ones to choose from.

In brief:

- Your puppy should **always** be supervised; otherwise he can harm himself or your home by ingesting something he shouldn't.

- To a dog, the world is a big toy box filled with toys he needs to try out. This even includes electrical wires and other harmful substances.

- **Always** have a leash attached so you can correct your pup immediately before he ingests and swallows something harmful or runs from you.

The leash and collar enable you to correct him in a manner he instinctively understands.

- Say "no" and at the same time issue a firm but gentle leash correction.
- Immediately follow a correction with praise.
- Never elevate the pack status of your dog by allowing him on furniture or the bed.

CRATE

There is a big controversy about using a crate. The dog is a pack animal and the pack provides safety and security. When your dog cannot be with you, a crate provides this same sense of safety and security.

So a crate is a necessary as well as humane training tool. It reinforces the dog's natural den instinct and offers a sense of security when he must be by himself.

Did you ever notice how a dog will sometimes go under a desk, table, or other small dark enclosed place? It's like being in a den or cave.

A crate is a temporary training tool that also increases your dog's ability to control going to the bathroom and ensures his safety as well as that of your home.

Once your dog respects you and feels secure in his environment – your home – you can wean him out of the crate, but not until he is at least nine to eleven months old.

Your dog may reach this point sooner or later, depending on his personality and your consistency with training.

A crate should never be used as a punishment tool. Your dog must have only a positive association with the crate.

Food and water should not be available to your dog in the crate.

If he gets bored or stressed or stimulated by the mailman, the UPS driver, or neighbors walking by, this could case him to eat or drink. Then he needs to urinate because he is unable to hold it. Eventually he gets used to being in his own mess.

Wolves have different places where they eat, sleep, and relieve themselves. You want to be consistent with your dog's natural pack instincts.

Fifteen minutes prior to putting your dog in the crate, he should be with you but get no attention from you.

When you are going to leave, calmly lead your dog to the crate and put him in. You can throw a small kibble of food or a treat in.

Although I find it unnecessary and unhealthy to train with food, in this case you are creating a positive association with the crate and the food has nothing to do with you.

If you lavish attention on your dog before you put him in there and then leave, you are traumatizing your dog and could possibly promote separation anxiety.

The same is true when you come home. Briefly greet your dog, put on his leash and take him to do his bathroom duties.

Then keep him with you, but go about your normal routine for five or ten minutes. Only then should you lavish attention on your dog.

If your coming or going becomes an emotional, daily high point for your dog, he will feel stressed when you are not there.

If your coming and going is no big deal, he will still be glad to see you when you get home, but he will be more secure when you are not there.

I have already said that until your dog is reliably trained, he should have absolutely **zero** unsupervised freedom in your home. Yes, I mean that literally.

But let's be realistic. Who can put her life on hold for the dog?

So I recommend establishing a "place" in every room of your home. A "place" is not a punishment nor is it ever used as such. It is a designated spot or area where you can see your dog and he can see you, but where you have control and he is secure.

You can have ten places in a room – it does not have to be the same spot every time.

The same applies with "place" as with the crate. If your dog is not housebroken and you give him too much space, instinctively he will do his business in one area, then go into another to lie down or play as he does not like to be in his own mess.

The crate must be small enough so that the dog has enough room to be comfortable but not enough to make a mess in one end and sleep in the other.

This is important until he develops control and can handle more room without seeing it as part of a bathroom area.

He does not know when and where he is supposed to relieve himself, so you need to teach him.

Confining his space until he is housebroken should go hand in hand with fitting him into his new pack where there is no option for bad behavior.

Make sure your puppy is well exercised and tired before being placed, otherwise it is frustrating for him.

Also make sure he has toys or bones so he has something to do and does not look upon place as a punishment.

He should only be in place where you can see him and he can see you. NEVER leave your dog in place and go out of the room, even for ONE SECOND. It could be one second too many, literally.

Nor should you leave him in place when another person wants to interact with him.

Here's how to teach place: Take the leash, and as you lead your dog to his "place," you point the entire way. At the same time, in a happy, jovial tone, repeat "place, place, place."

Only good things happen in "place" in order to reinforce a positive association.

You should pre-tie inexpensive nylon leashes in convenient areas of your home. Make sure he has only eight to ten inches of leash.

If you give him the whole length of the leash, he will not understand "place" as that one exact spot. A two- to four-foot vicinity is too much.

You have to be literal and teach the dog exactly what you want. You want to reinforce that you are in control everywhere in the home.

This also inhibits your dog's ability to go relieve himself just anywhere and then move to another area, so it helps with housebreaking.

If you leave your dog gated in another part of the house you are using good intentions but bad judgment.

Because you feel bad and want him to have more freedom, you are doing

the opposite of what you are intending. You are actually stressing your dog by giving him too much freedom too soon.

A crate reinforces a dog's natural instincts of safety and security when he is unable to be with his pack.

When you are at home, if it is at all possible, he should be with you and not kept in the crate. "Place" allows you to accomplish this from day one without him having accidents or chewing what he shouldn't.

He doesn't understand why he can't be with you. He is, after all, a pack animal and you are his pack.

He needs to learn how to fit into your entire house, but now you can control him and minimize his ability to have an accident.

Tying is only temporary until your pup learns what "place" means. Make sure he has toys to occupy him.

Now he is in the room where you are and you are teaching him how life is going to be.

When you are cooking, eating, or cleaning up, your dog should never be near the "top dog's kill," that is, your food.

It is inconsistent with his natural instincts and prevents him from developing bad habits like stealing food or having people slip him table food.

Furthermore, if your dog is underfoot while you are cooking in the kitchen or near or at the stove, you and he could get hurt.

As long as he can see you and you can see him, he is still part of the "pack" but you are now teaching him how life is going to be in *your* "pack."

If you are consistent, eventually you will not have to tie your dog; just point and say, "place," and he will go to the designated spot.

How consistent and repetitious you are determines how quickly your dog "gets it." And if you are consistent, he will get it.

Never – and I cannot stress the word **never** enough – leave your dog tied, even for **one second** and leave the room. Either take him with you or put him in the crate if you must leave that area.

If you leave your dog tied and alone, it creates stress and frustration and even aggression. And, he learns to dislike "place."

Again, tying him is only to each him. You want him to like it. Even if he falls asleep, wake him up. His senses are much stronger than ours and he will hear you leave and will be awake.

When he is "in place" it is quiet time. Children should be taught that a dog can not be turned off and on like a light switch.

It is unfair to get a puppy all wound up and then to just stop. He can't.

Place is an area and time for your dog to be quiet and controlled for those moments when your family is eating breakfast, lunch, dinner, or snacks, as well as when you or your family want to watch TV, read, do homework, or whatever.

You must teach your dog how to fit into your lifestyle at your schedule and convenience.

Run your dog outside before he will be "in place" as exercise will stimulate him to go to the bathroom.

This will help to ensure that he is on empty so that he is better able to be quiet for a longer period of time, giving you and your family the down time you need.

When in doubt, if he yelps, whimpers, barks, or cries, take him out to go to the bathroom.

If you know he is on empty, tell him "no" one time. And if he does not stop, do not repeat your "no." Instead, casually and calmly walk to your pup, grab him by the back of the collar so his head doesn't move and administer something orally distasteful. Undiluted white vinegar in a spray bottle usually does the trick.

You want to make sure you have the nozzle between his lips so you don't accidentally spray him in the face or eyes; and just a little taste, not a full squeeze on the bottle.

It may take a couple of repetitions but your dog will see the pattern and learn to respond when you say "no."

You want your dog to listen the first time every time, so do not repeat your correction. Do not say "no" more than once and then correct.

Make sure your dog is not just coming out of the crate all energized and then put in place; he will be bouncing off the walls. He needs to be kept tired.

Put a long lead on your puppy, take him outside, throw the ball and exercise him! He needs to be kept tired so he can comfortably stay in place and chew on some toys. A tired dog means a happy owner!

When you are outdoors, do not take the leash off your dog unless you have a *reliably* off-leash-trained dog.

The dog you have at the beginning is *not* what you will have in a couple weeks.

As his instincts develop and mature he is going to want to explore, not to mention if a cat or squirrel runs by and he reacts and gives chase.

You won't be able to catch your dog when he bolts unless you have a long leash on him and you can control him by grabbing the leash.

It only takes that one time. Every time you remove the leash you are gambling with your dog's life, and possibly someone else's safety and your liability.

Yes, you are responsible for your dog, so keep him and everyone else safe.

If you want to run your dog off-leash, you must fence in your property or get your dog reliably trained off-leash. Only then can you be sure that even with a cat running right under his nose and him taking off after it, you can make your dog respond immediately on command to return to you.

That is the control necessary for off-leash walking. If you are not absolutely sure, then you have no business not having a leash on your dog.

"Place" should *only* be used when you and your family are eating, cooking, cleaning up food, or otherwise working, and after the dog has been exercised.

These are times when you cannot devote your full attention to him but want to teach him how to fit into your family routine in every area of your house.

It is not needed when you or another family member has the ability to interact and completely focus on the dog.

Place should always be down low, for example, around the leg at the bottom of a piece of furniture. This way if the puppy tries to jump or lunge, he corrects himself.

Tying him to a doorknob affords too much room and enables him to jump and lunge on kids or people walking by.

Place affords you the ability to have your dog with you everywhere in your home.

Being in place and with you is far less stressful than him being in a crate in another part of the house.

In brief:

- Never use a crate as a punishment. Place your dog in his crate **only** when you are not home and cannot watch him.

- Avoid emotional goodbyes or hellos which promote separation anxiety.

- The crate must be big enough that your dog can be comfortable standing, lying down, and stretching.

SOCIALIZATION

Let's talk about socialization for your puppy.

First, for health reasons your dog should be completely inoculated before interacting with other dogs.

Second, your dog should be socialized *daily* – yes, *every day*.

Dogs need mental stimulation every day or they get bored, frustrated, or destructive.

Socialization means seeing other dogs, people, kids, cars, bikes, joggers, etc., but under your supervision and control and *not* by letting every dog and person approach and pet your dog. If you allow this to occur you are sending the wrong message to your dog.

A dog is not, nor should he ever be, friendly to everyone. A dog is an animal and is supposed to be instinctively leery of unfamiliar people and other dogs.

As I said earlier, you wouldn't allow a stranger to approach and hug your small child. The same is true for your pet.

When you let strangers and dogs approach, the message your dog receives is that he is the one deciding where and if this new "dog" fits into his pack (yes, just you and your dog is a pack to a dog) and only the alpha, lead dog of the pack makes decisions.

Inadvertently you look weak to your dog. And now you have taught your dog that he has the *right* to meet and greet everyone – just the opposite of your wanting him to remain controlled and well-behaved even when distracted.

Many people adopt dogs from other people, rescue groups, or shelters. They are not aware of potential bad behaviors, such as dog aggression, that their new pet may be coming with until he reacts to *your* dog.

For all these reasons, dogs need to see other dogs, people, cars, joggers, etc., but under your control so that your dog is exposed to real life in a controlled manner that is safe for both you and him.

A tight leash telegraphs stress from you to your dog. A better way is to put your foot on the leash so you have

immediate full control. That way, if the dog starts to jump he will correct himself. This is effortless for you and calming for your dog.

Remember, a jumping dog is showing dominance, not excitability. He is trying, as Mother Nature intended, to dominate the approaching person.

As I recommended before, just say, "Please do not approach my dog, he is in training."

I have found that people are very responsive to that. And even if they are offended, I prefer not to put my dog or myself, or them, in a bad situation by allowing them to pet my dog even for ten seconds.

Remember, *you* are responsible for your dog and his actions, and your dog will pay the ultimate and costly price for your irresponsibility.

In brief:

- Take daily walks, always varying the route.
- Place your foot on the leash, with your dog on the outside of your foot, when people or dogs are approaching.
- Tell people not to approach or let their dog approach since your dog is in training.
- When your dog is calm, remove your foot from the leash and allow the other dog to approach, if you so desire.
- If or when your dog acts inappropriately, say a firm "no" at the same time as you tug on the leash.

- Immediately give praise after correction to teach your dog what you want and expect.
- If your dog repeats bad behavior, repeat the correction until he learns.
- Do not pet or allow your dog to be petted when acting inappropriately as it will only reinforce behavior.
- To your pet, touching equals praise, and even negative attention is attention. So you only want to acknowledge your dog, either verbally or physically, when your foot is off the leash and he is calm.
- This teaches him the wanted behavior. He will see a pattern and learn that when he is calm he gets what he most desires: your praise.
- A hyper dog is a stressed dog; a calm dog is a secure dog.

HOUSEBREAKING

There is a formula for housebreaking. The first step is what you are already doing which is controlling your dog's environment.

Eight-week-old puppies usually have to urinate about every two hours. If there is any additional stimulation such as a person arriving at the house, or playing, they will have to go again even if it is before the two-hour mark.

When in doubt, take your dog out.

Have the crate placed near the door you will be using for housebreaking. I recommend that you use one specific door to take the dog to go to the bathroom.

For walking, playing, and so on, the door does not matter, but you want your puppy to see a set pattern for housebreaking and which door is used to go to the bathroom.

Do not get up every few hours at night to take your dog out as this is simply conditioning him to get up too often.

If you hear your puppy crying or barking, take him outside. As soon as he relieves himself, take him right back into the house, and right back into the crate.

If you play with him, or cuddle him, he learns this as part of a pattern in the middle of the night.

Dogs are able to "hold it" much sooner through the night versus during the day as there are less stimuli at night such as the mailman, other dogs, kids getting out of school, etc.

Your pup's crate should be in your room at night so he hears your breathing and tossing and turning.

This makes him feel more secure by being with the pack and not isolated, adding to his ability to gain more control sooner throughout the night by minimizing his stress.

The second step is to teach your dog to give you a signal to let you know he has to go out.

Put some bells tied to rope, ribbon, or twine, low enough where your puppy can bat them or swat them without jumping up, to teach your dog how to give you a signal.

Only ring the bells to take your dog right to the "spot" you are going to designate for him to go to the bathroom.

Ringing the bells while saying "out boy! out boy!" in a happy and jovial manner reinforces a positive association with the bells and going out to the bathroom.

Do not use the bells for playing, walking, or correcting. You want him to distinctly associate bells with bathroom only!

You should go through the door first, whether entering or exiting your home, as you are the "alpha" dog. You then lead your dog right to the spot you designate for his bathroom area.

Let your dog have as much leash as you desire but don't let him lead you around to pick and choose where he wants to go.

When you teach your dog to go in this one area or spot, this is the only area or spot your dog will go to when you take or let him out for the bathroom for the rest of his life. However, you must be consistent until he doesn't *want* to go anywhere else.

Remember, it is all about conditioning. You want and need to be specific as to *exactly* what you want.

This makes cleanup easier and your kids and company will not be bringing the mess into your house because it will always be contained.

The third step is to teach your dog to go on command.

While your puppy is doing his business, whether he is urinating or defecating, consistently repeat your command – for example "hurry up, hurry up, hurry up" – the entire time your dog is eliminating.

He will learn to associate going to the bathroom with whatever you are saying, enabling you to get your dog to go on command.

A puppy is very easily distracted by any little thing such as a bird singing or a leaf blowing.

Even in the middle of peeing, a puppy will become overwhelmed with the distraction and stop mid-stream, then remember he didn't finish when he gets back inside, and do it instead in your home.

Make sure your puppy has more than one opportunity to go when you are outside to ensure he is on empty.

A male dog always leaves a little on reserve so he needs to have more than one opportunity to eliminate.

When your puppy has finished, give him resounding praise, making him believe he has just accomplished the greatest feat in the world.

The fourth step is scheduling your puppy's food and water.

Food and water should *not* be kept in the crate. The dog's crate represents his "den" and he should not eat where he sleeps, just as he should not go to the bathroom where he sleeps unless he has been kept in those conditions and has become accustomed to that. But that is a behavioral problem and not the instinctive norm.

Dogs will not dry up on you or starve to death in the crate for a couple of hours.

Up to six months of age they need to be fed three times a day, with access to food and water for 20-30 minutes during those times.

After the designated 20-30 minutes, pick up your dog's food and water. It will make your dog more consistent at eating when and while it is available. He learns that "you snooze, you lose," so eat while you can.

You could put your dog in an area where you are visible to each other so you can go about your routine while keeping him on a feeding schedule.

You need to know when the food and water are "going in" so you can determine when it may be "coming out."

Your dog will need access to water more than the designated three times a day, but by knowing exactly when he ingested something you can minimize accidents and accelerate housebreaking.

At six months of age you can cut out the midday feeding and keep your dog on a twice daily feeding schedule.

If your dog is on a low quality food that is high in fillers, he will have to go more frequently since his system will have to pass through what he cannot use. A high quality food will produce less stool.

Wet food should not be given unless your vet prescribes it for specific medical conditions.

Wetting your dog's dry food expands it so your puppy is not getting the recommended nutritional amount and does not give the teeth the workout they need to remain clean and strong.

The fifth step in housebreaking is correction. This correction can and must be done even if it is after the fact so your dog does not condition himself to go in your house.

There must be consequences for inappropriate behavior or your dog will not be able to see and learn the cause and effect.

Your dog's scent is very clear to him. So even if you did not catch your dog having an accident, you know you didn't do it.

You calmly lead your dog to the accident, by the leash, and then take the collar and bring your dog's nose close to the accident, but *not* in it. He can smell it and the last thing you want to do is reinforce your dog being *in* his mess.

As you bring his nose to the accident, in a firm voice you tell him, "bad boy." Do not yell or use his name as you will lose the benefit of him directly associating the correction with his behavior.

Have a spray bottle with white vinegar with you so immediately after your bring his mess to his attention and tell him, "bad boy," you bring the nozzle of the spray bottle to his lips, making sure you get the nozzle in between the lips so you do not spray his face or eyes. Give him a little taste of the white vinegar.

You want to hold your dog by the collar so he cannot move his face, ensuring that the vinegar goes in his mouth and no place else. No, do not dilute the white vinegar. You are not giving your puppy a *full* spray of it, just a taste.

Immediately after you administer the vinegar, take your dog to his outside place.

Do not ring the bell since this is not happy time but a correction, so you can reinforce where your dog should have gone and needs to go in the future.

His scent is already there so he will have a good idea what is going on.

Then you take him back inside and clean the accident area up with nothing but straight white vinegar.

Do not let your dog see you clean up his mess since this would look submissive to him.

The vinegar will neutralize the scent and is actually used as a cleanser, but it will also enable you to create the negative association with your dog inappropriately relieving himself in your house.

There have to be consequences for inappropriate behavior or your dog will never know any better.

In brief:

- Control your dog's environment.
- Teach your dog to signal his need to go to the bathroom.
- Teach your dog to go on command.
- Schedule his food and water.
- Create a negative association for inappropriately relieving himself in your home.

GENERAL INFORMATION

Everything I am going over in this book is in preparation for a formal obedience program.

The basic commands – heel, sit, stay, come, down – are ready to be started between the ages of 12-16 weeks depending on the breed.

This is so that by the time a dog is 6-9 months old and hitting the adolescent "testing" stage, the owner knows what to do and how to do it, and will not allow the dog to develop any bad habits or behaviors.

If you lay a firm foundation as to who is in charge and the dominant "alpha" dog while your dog is going through adolescence, you can enjoy a well-behaved, well-mannered pet for the rest of his life with you.

If you have a linked chain and one link is weak, the entire chain is useless.

You need to provide your dog with the structure, boundaries, and limitations of your "pack." If not, your efforts are only counter-productive.

Your dog will behave badly and in the end will pay the ultimate price by either being eliminated from interaction with you or by being put outside or placed in a shelter. *You* have a responsibility to your dog.

Showing love to your dog through excessive petting and spoiling throughout adolescence does both you and your pet a disservice. Excessive petting equals excessive praise.

Once he is past the age of adolescence, as long as you have established, maintained, and reinforced your leadership, your dog is able to understand your love as a perk and not his right.

Let me address the "I got the dog for the children" statement I have heard so often.

Please understand that although this may be the case, mom, dad, *you* are going to have the work of the dog.

It is that simple. If you make training fun, as it should be for you and the dog, then the will kids *want* to be involved and it is not just another chore.

The three F's of dog training:

1. **Fun** – Training should be fun, not just for you but also for your dog. Dogs are very intelligent, yet very simple. They need to be taught what you want from them so they can

123

please you. They do not come pre-programmed.

2. Fair – Training should be fair for the dog. Just like a child, dogs need commitment, consistency, repetition, and kindness. Remember, you are the teacher and the dog is the student. You must have the time and patience necessary to teach your animal.

3. Firm – Your dog needs tough love, firm structure, and strict boundaries. That is how you show love to your dog. It makes him feel secure, calm, and happy.

There is no such thing as a "bad dog." Either through predisposed genetic mishap (which is rare) or, more commonly, through its environment and poor training, a dog may become misbehaved, or worse, aggressive.

There are different types of aggression: dominance, fear, possessive, protective, predatory, inter-gender, pain-elicited, punishment-elicited, maternal, redirected, touch-sensitive.

You want to hire a behavior specialist who is recommended by reliable dog community personnel.

The type of aggression needs to be determined so that the behavior modification program with the best chance of success can be implemented.

Dogs are fundamentally the same, hence so is the basis of training. That having been said, every dog's personality is unique and what works for one dog may not necessarily work for another.

A behavior specialist should be able, after an evaluation with you and your dog, to determine why your dog is exhibiting poor behavior and come up with a program to correct it.

Currently there are no guidelines to identify what is a "behavior specialist" or a "trainer." A person can have one week's experience or ten years and yet have the same title.

Referrals should come from reliable dog personnel such as vets' offices, kennels, groomers, or other clients.

You should check into the history, experience, and methods of the behaviorist.

Private training, starting in the dog's own environment and neighborhood, then progressing to more distracting environments is most realistic.

If your pup does not listen to you in his own environment, how can you possibly expect him to listen in a more distracting one?

AGGRESSION

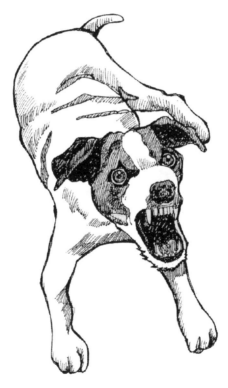

A GROWL IS A BITE THAT DID NOT CONNECT!

Let me state this again.

NO MATTER WHAT YOU WANT TO THINK, OR WHAT EXCUSES YOU WANT TO MAKE FOR YOUR DOG'S BEHAVIOR, YOUR DOG GROWLING IS A BITE THAT DID NOT CONNECT!

A growl is a warning from one dog to another. Unless nipped in the bud, a growl will progress to lifting of the lip, showing the teeth, air bite, and then a connection.

It is nothing personal from the dog's perspective; it is how his world works.

A growl needs to be treated like a bite, and an immediate training program needs to be instituted to reinforce your pet's lower rank in his pack. Once he respects you, he will respect what is associated with you, such as your house and your children.

Breed does *not* guarantee a dog's behavior, and if a dog has teeth he is capable of biting.

You must never lose sight of the fact that your dog is a pack animal first, dog second, and your pet third.

Fear aggression is one of the most misunderstood types of aggression, in my opinion.

When a puppy or dog acts fearful, it is human instinct to console the dog and make him feel better by petting and coddling him.

You are inadvertently reinforcing the behavior by praising the dog while he is afraid and escalating his fearfulness.

Do not touch your dog when he is acting afraid.

Depending on the situation, there are different ways of dealing with the fear.

For example, with loud noises such as thunder, do the jolly routine. Divert your dog's attention by taking out his favorite toy, and talk to him firmly but happily – not in a high-pitched baby voice – all in a positive manner.

You can set your dog up for getting used to the stimulus he is fearful of.

At different times of the day, on different days, drop a pot or a lid. When your dog reacts, be happy and jovial to desensitize him to loud noises.

With thunder, you might purchase a thunderstorm CD and play it daily at louder volumes and different times while doing something positive with your dog. Do this until you have de-sensitized him to thunder.

When people approach or come to the door, or in more distracting environments, your dog needs to feel secure.

Your first action should be putting your foot on the leash to make your dog deal with the situation and not add to his stress.

In this way he is causing the tension, and not you, which defines how he perceives any situation.

Remember, a tight leash reinforces a stressful situation. With your foot on the leash you have full control and your dog has no option but to settle down.

SUMMARY

Congratulations on the choice of your dog. I hope the information in this book starts your dog off on the right paw as far as who is in charge.

Using it, you will establish a firm foundation for a more formal basic obedience program that will encompass both daily indoor *and* outdoor reinforcement.

This includes leash behavior (heeling at your side), sits, stays, the "come" command, and the "down" command.

Formal obedience training allows you to maintain and reinforce your position as the leader of your pack.

And by doing so, you will build a wonderful bond with your pet.

He will not develop any bad habits or behaviors, so you won't have any to fix.

He will know what you expect from him and how to fit into your lifestyle and schedule. But you will have played to his natural instincts. This works well for everyone, including your dog.

The commitment to your dog now will pay off for the duration of his life with you.

Remember, most unwanted behaviors start right in the home. To prevent them, your dog must see you as the leader in both his own home environment and more distracting locations.

A dog is a dog is a dog.

As much as he becomes a person to us, we *must* give him the consistency, repetition, time, exercise, and mental stimulation he needs in order to thrive as a new family member, or, as your dog sees it, with his new pack.

JOURNAL

The following pages are provided so that you can keep a record of your dog's history, have a quick reference regarding veterinary and other resources, and have an up-to-date reference regarding vaccinations, medications, etc.

Complete as much or as little as you wish. If you board your dog, hire a trainer or sitter, or change veterinary services, take this book along for reference.

DOG INFORMATION

Dog's Name _____

Breed _____

Mixed Breed _____

AKC Registered Name_____

AKC Registration Number_____

Sex_____

Color and Markings_____

Date of Birth_____Litter Number_____

Sire Name & Number _____

Dam Name & Number _____

Breeder Name_____

Date Sold or Delivered_____

Neutered / Spayed:___Yes___No

Rescue/Shelter Dog? _____

Dog Food Brand(s)

Special Medical Conditions/Medications

Special Personality Traits

Any foods or treats dog cannot have?

Known Allergies/Other Health Related Information

OWNER

Name_____

Address_____

City, State, Zip_____

Home Phone_____

Work Phone_____

Cell Phone_____

E-Mail_____

VETERINARIAN/HOSPITAL

Name_____

Clinic Name_____

Clinic Address_____

City, State, Zip_____

Phone_____

Emergecy Phone_____

Email_____

MEDICATION/INNOCULATION DATES:

Rabies License #_____

Date Rabies Shot_____

Date Distemper (DHHP) Shot_____

Date Bordatella Shot_____

Flea Preventative_____

Heartworm Medication_____

Dental Exam_____

VACCINATIONS

Distemper: Airborne viral disease of the lungs, intestines and brain.

Hepatitis: Viral disease of the liver.

Parainfluenza: Infectious bronchitis.

Parvovirus: Viral disease of the intestines.

Rabies: Viral disease fatal to humans and other animals.

Bordetella (also called Kennel Cough): Bacterial infection of the upper respiratory system.

The following is a basic vaccination guideline. Always consult your veterinarian before starting any treatment. Also, some states require rabies vaccinations every three years while others require them to be done annually.

DHPP: (Distemper, Hepatitis, Parainfluenza, Parvovirus): 6-8 weeks, 10-12 weeks, 14-16 weeks. Then at 1 year then every 3 years.

Rabies: Annually or as required by your state.

Bordetella: Optional every 6 or 12 months.

MEDICAL CONDITIONS, SUGERIES, INJURIES

Sometimes the unexpected happens and our pet gets injured or ill. Use this space for notes about any illnesses, surgeries, or injuries including medications and specific treatments.

DOG TRAINER

Name_____

Address_____

City, State, Zip_____

Home Phone_____

Work Phone_____

Cell Phone_____

E-Mail_____

DOG SITTER

Name_____

Address_____

City, State, Zip_____

Home Phone_____

Work Phone_____

Cell Phone_____

E-Mail_____

BOARDING KENNEL

Name_____

Address_____

City, State, Zip_____

Phone_____

E-Mail_____

NOTES

NOTES

NOTES

Made in the USA
Charleston, SC
11 May 2012